GRAYSCALE COLORING BOOK
WONDERFUL
Ladybugs
AND FLOWERS
ADULT COLORING BOOK

VOLUME 2.

PATTERNS FOR RELAXATION AND STRESS RELIEF

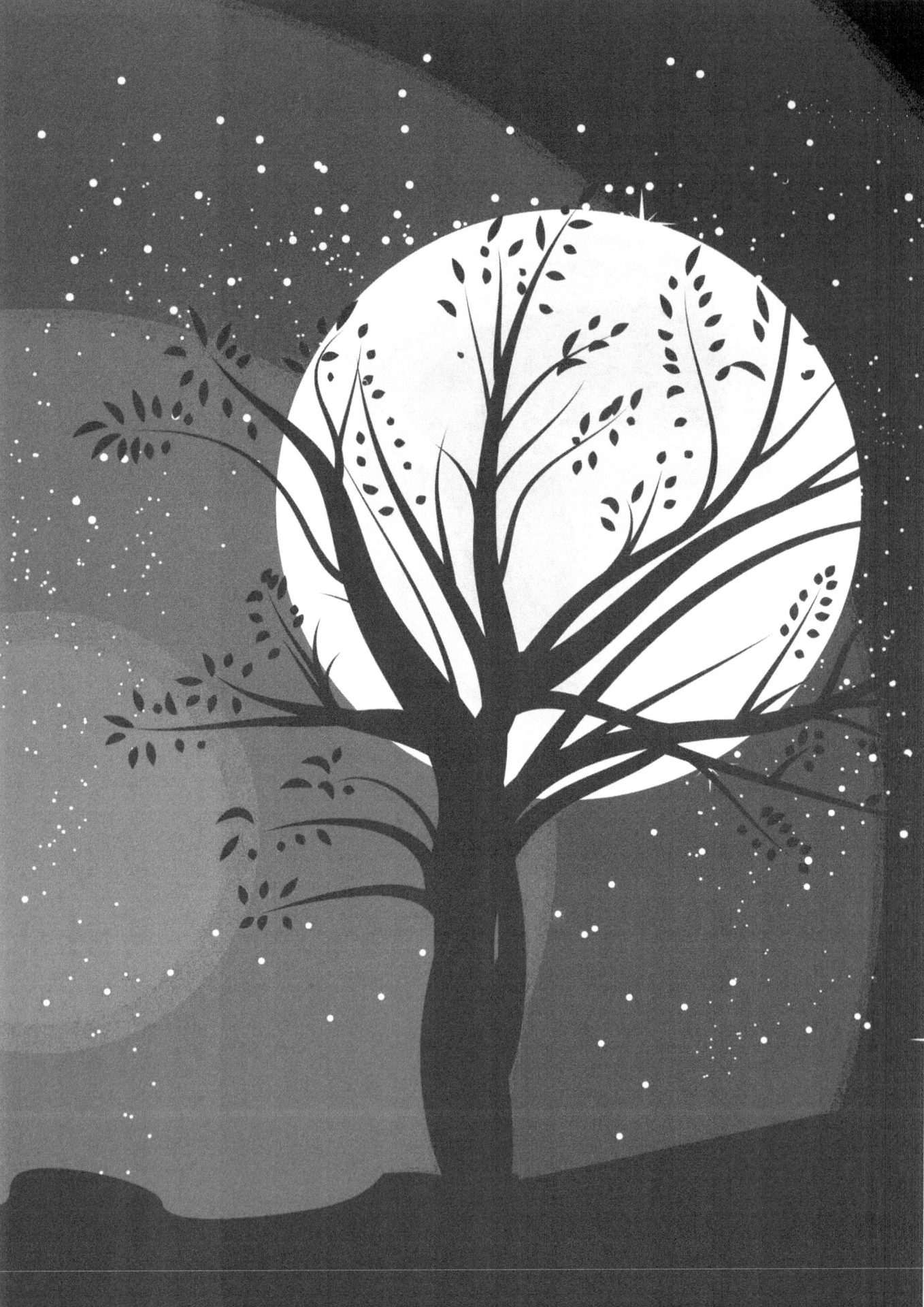

COLOR TEST PAGE

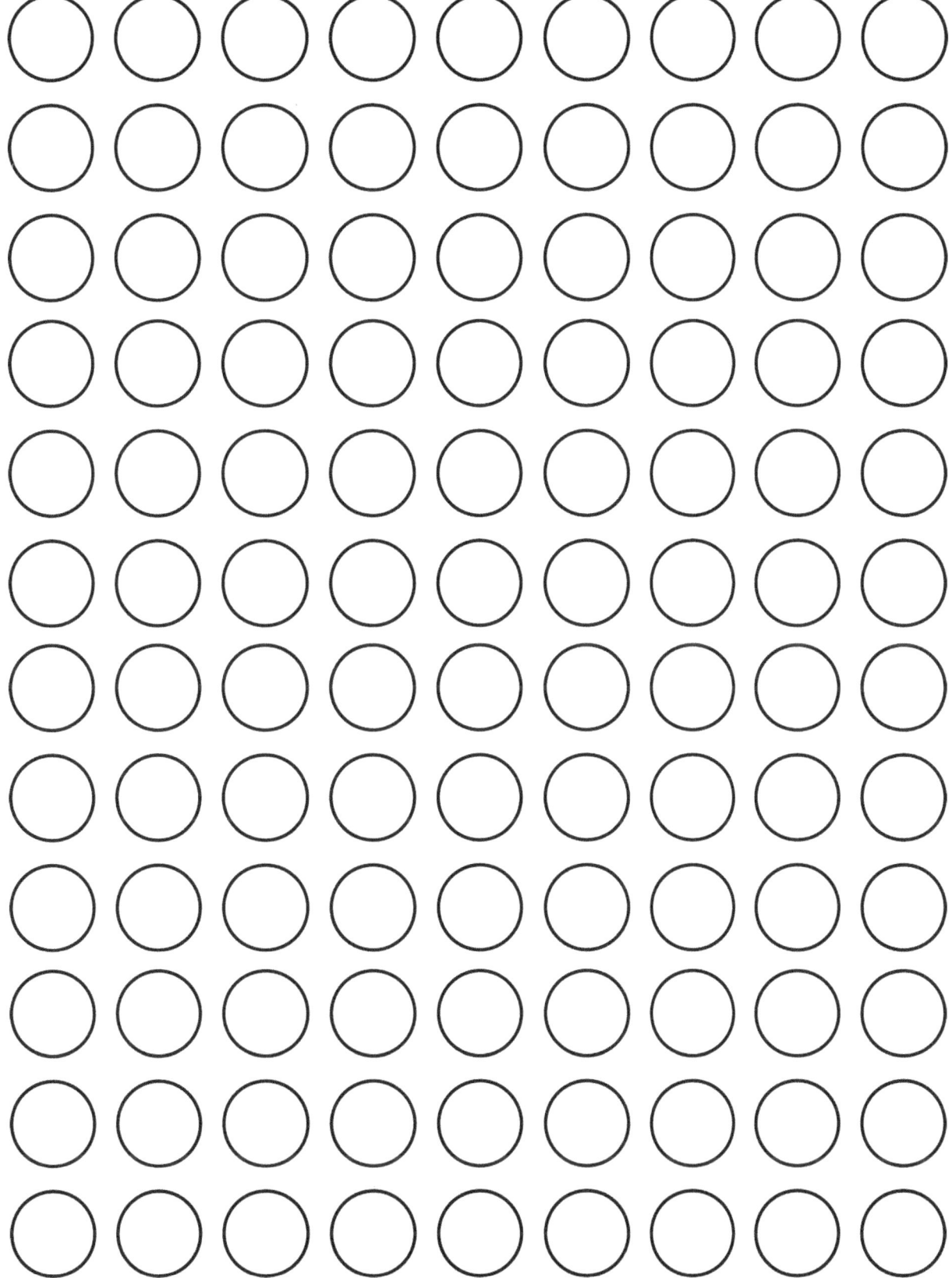

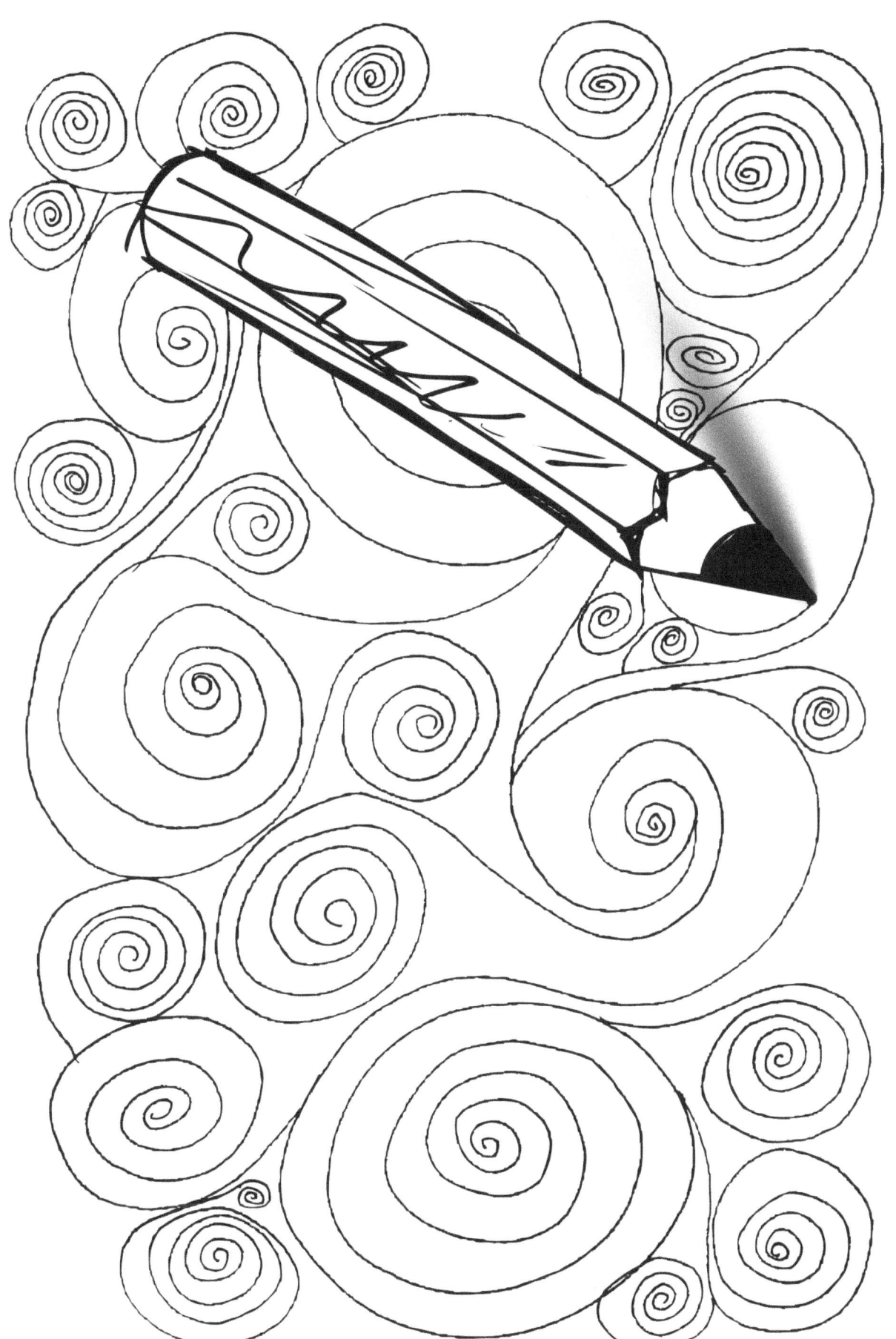

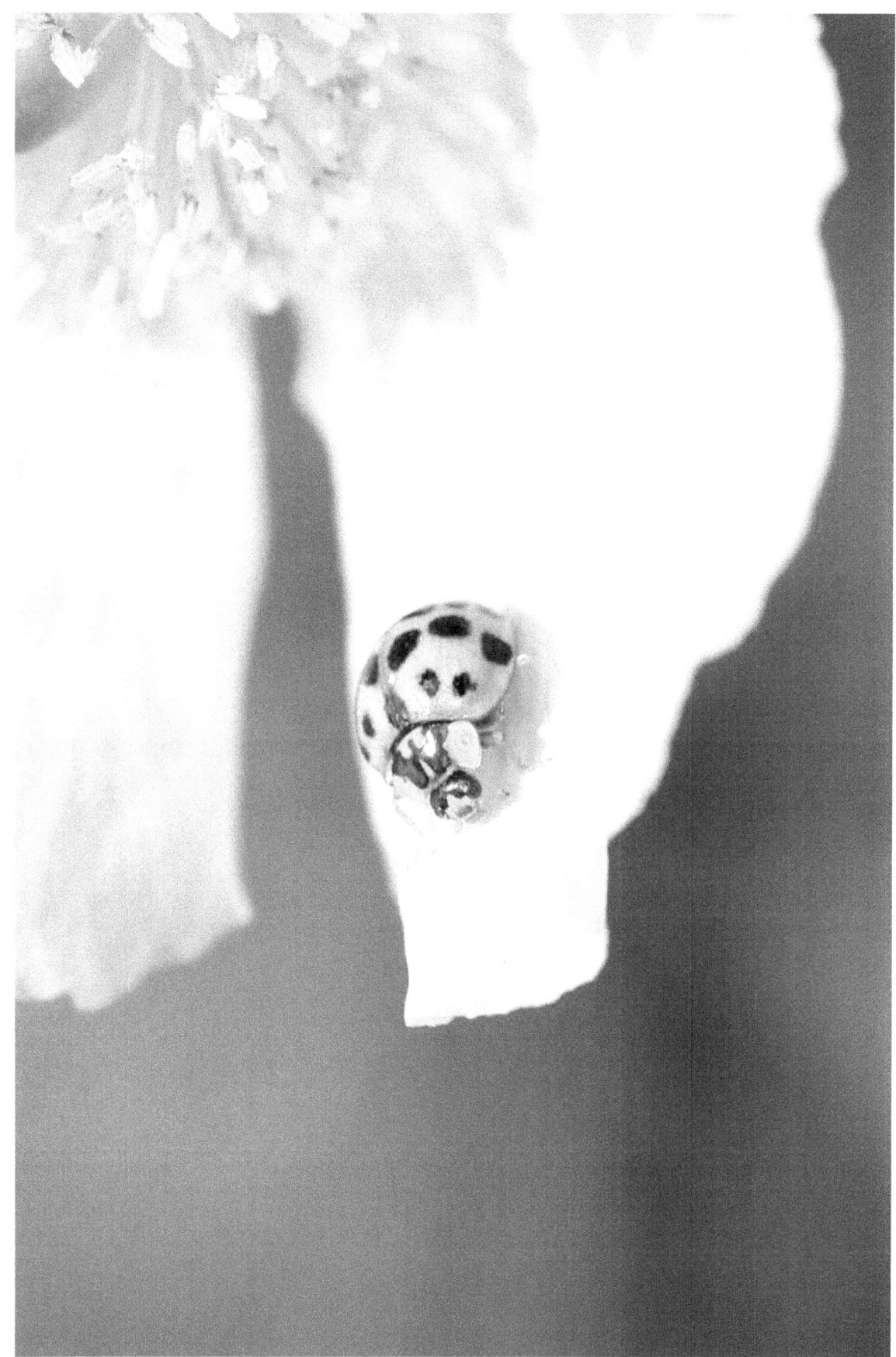

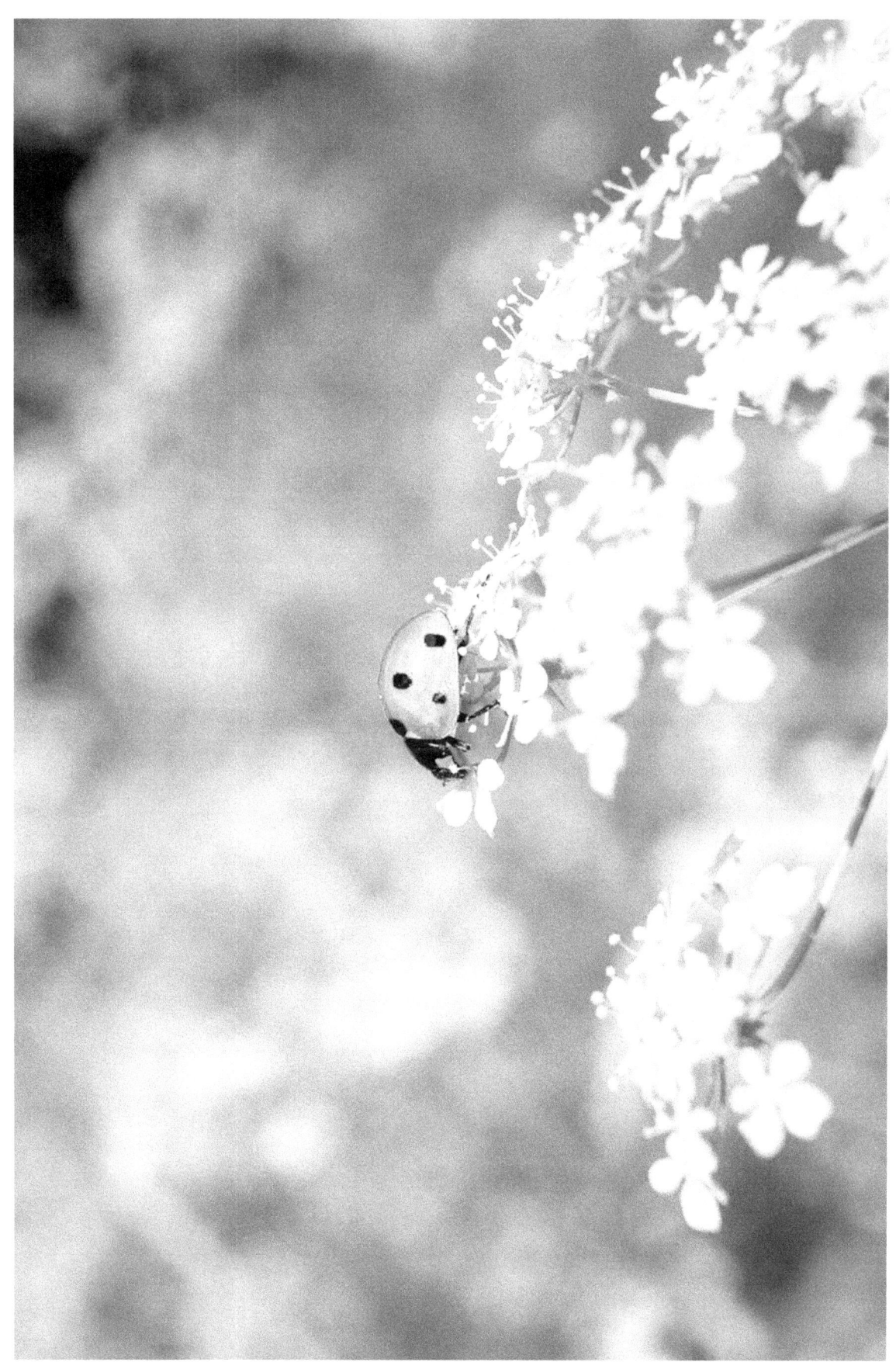

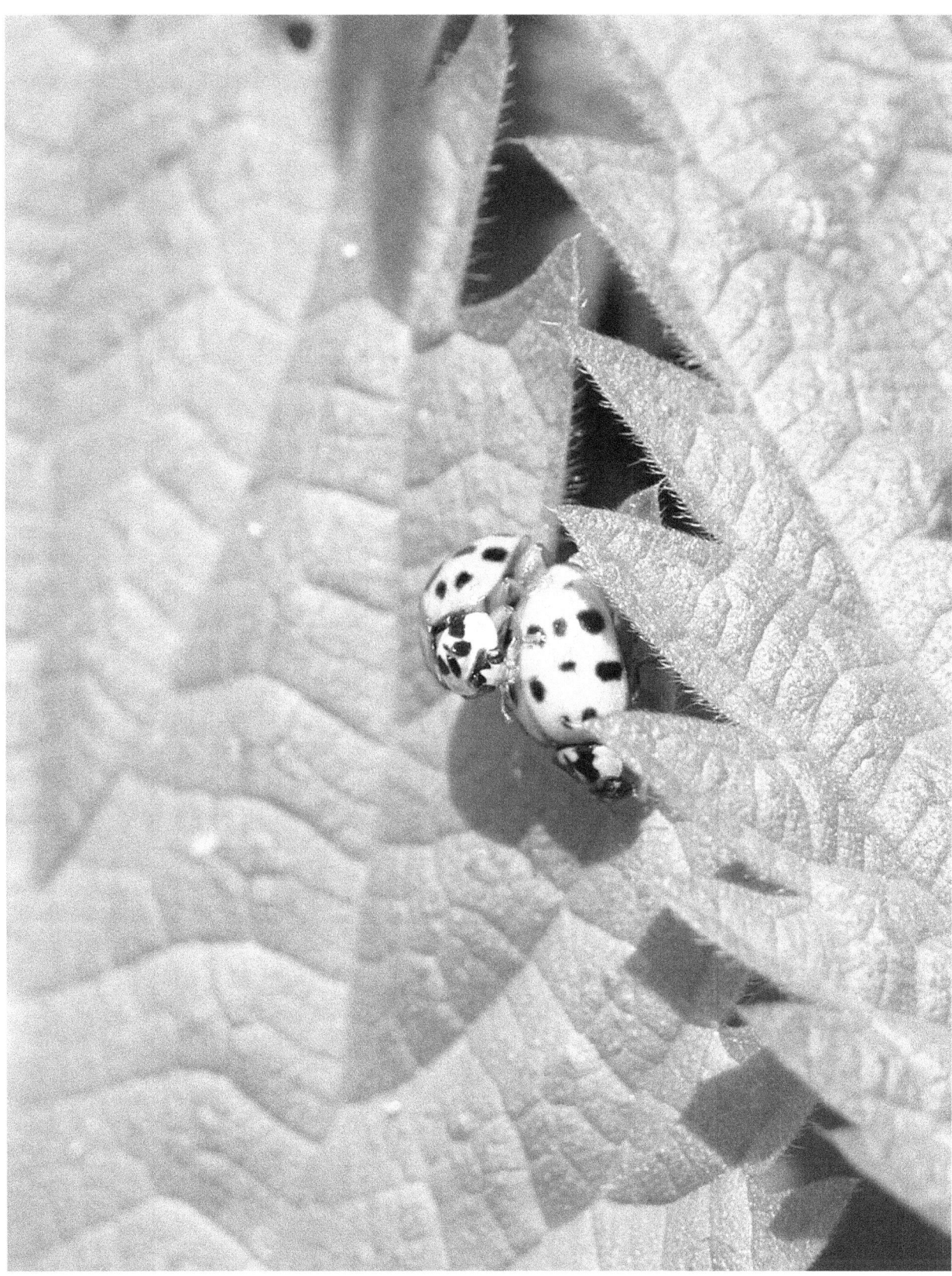

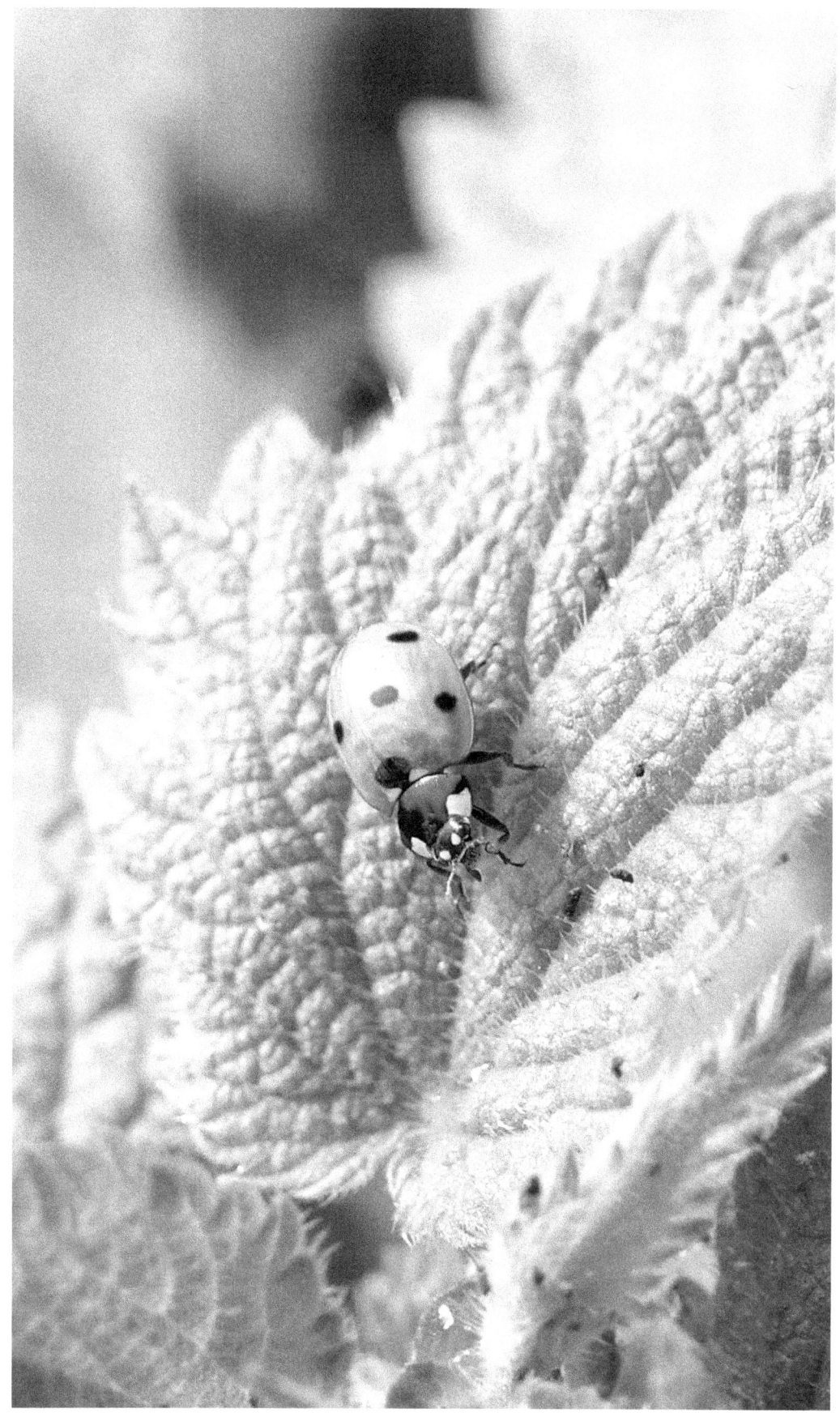

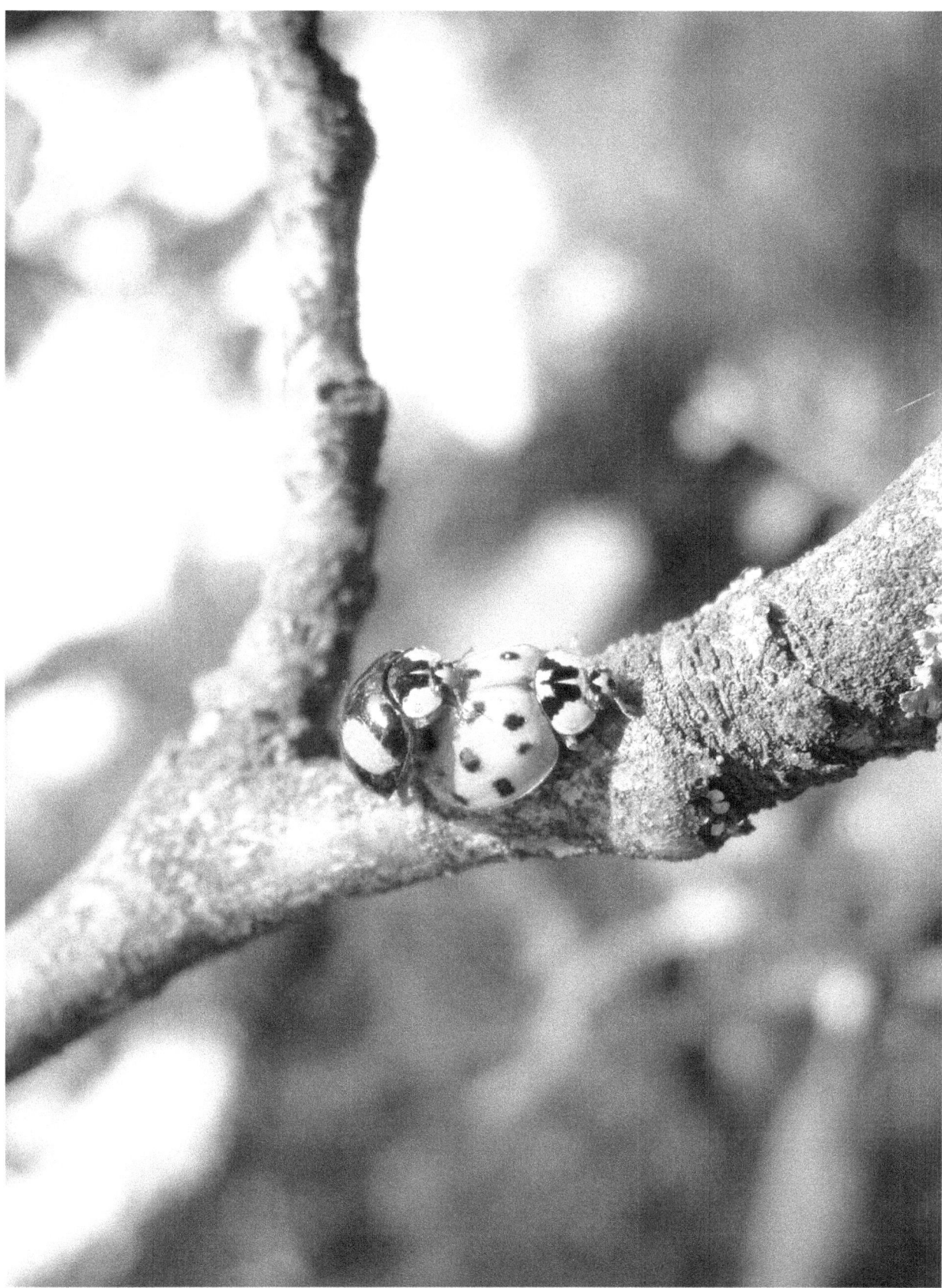

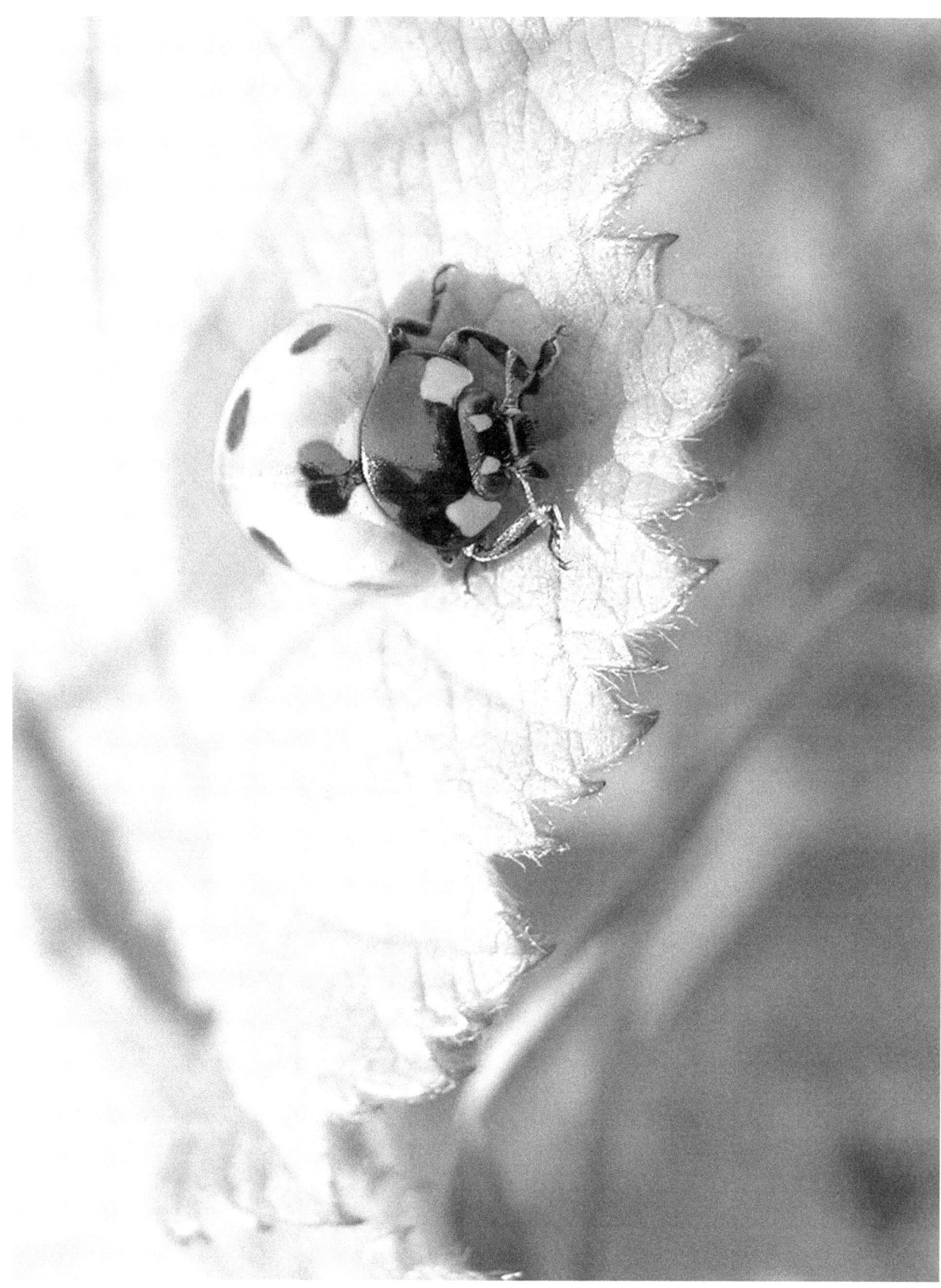

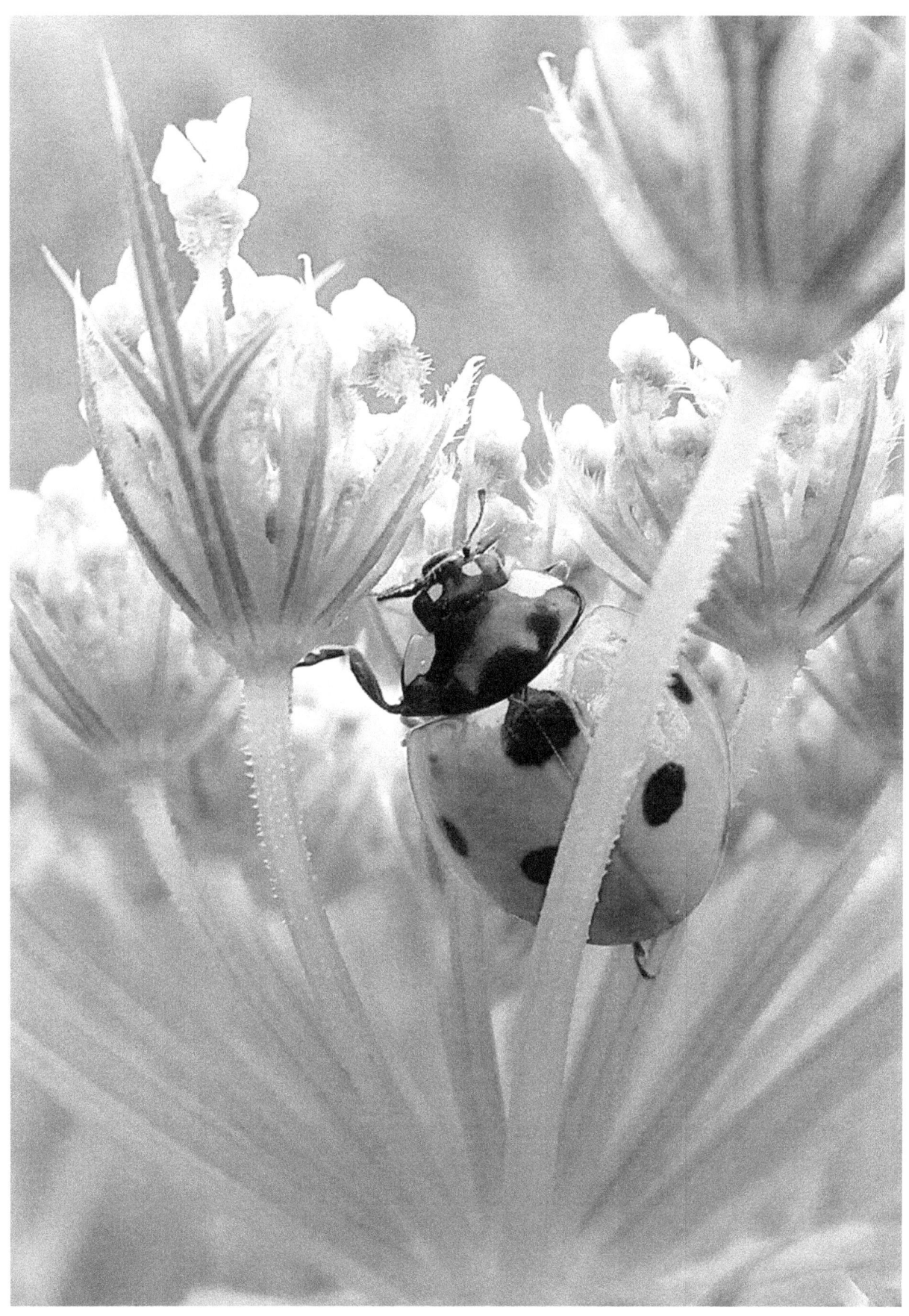

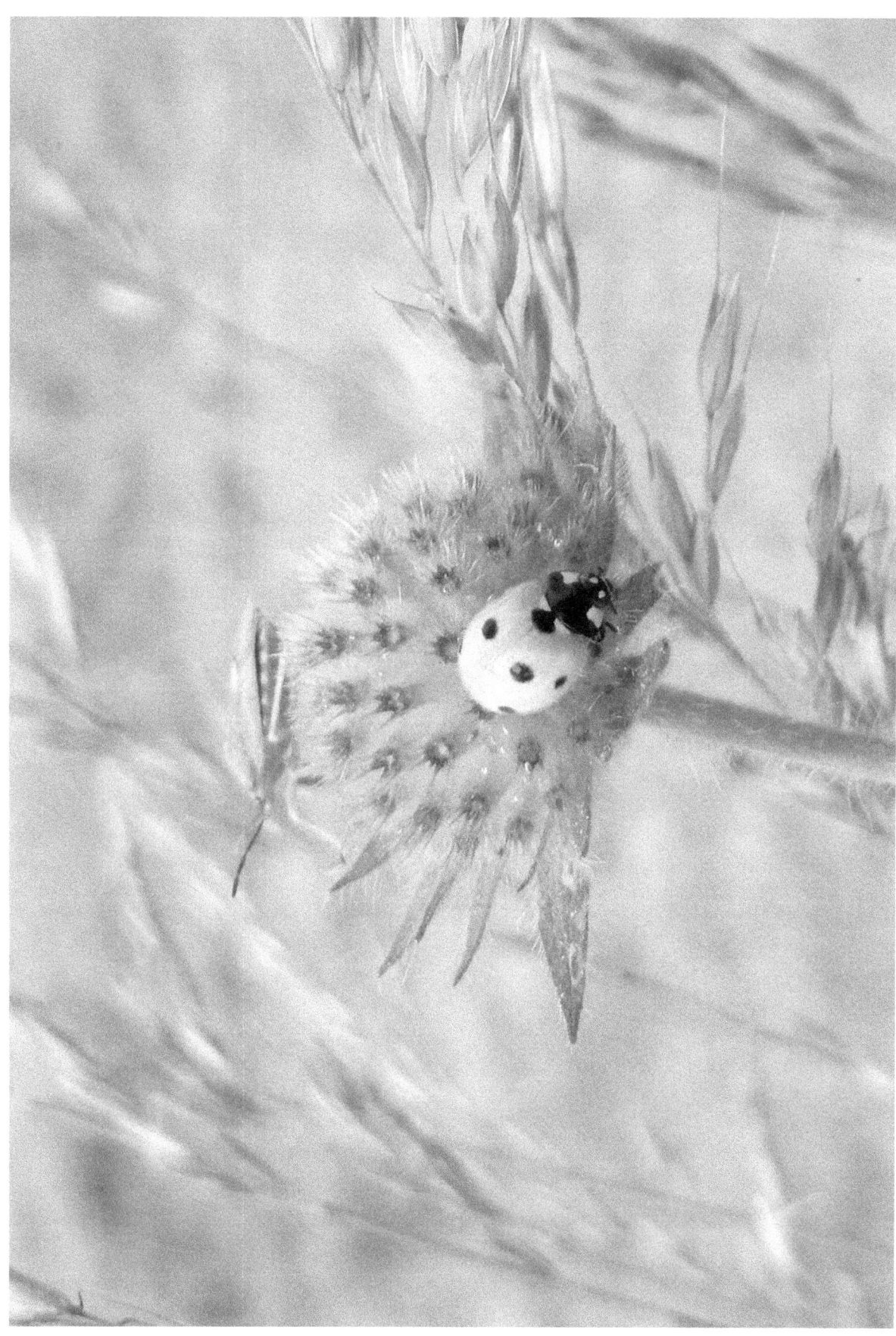

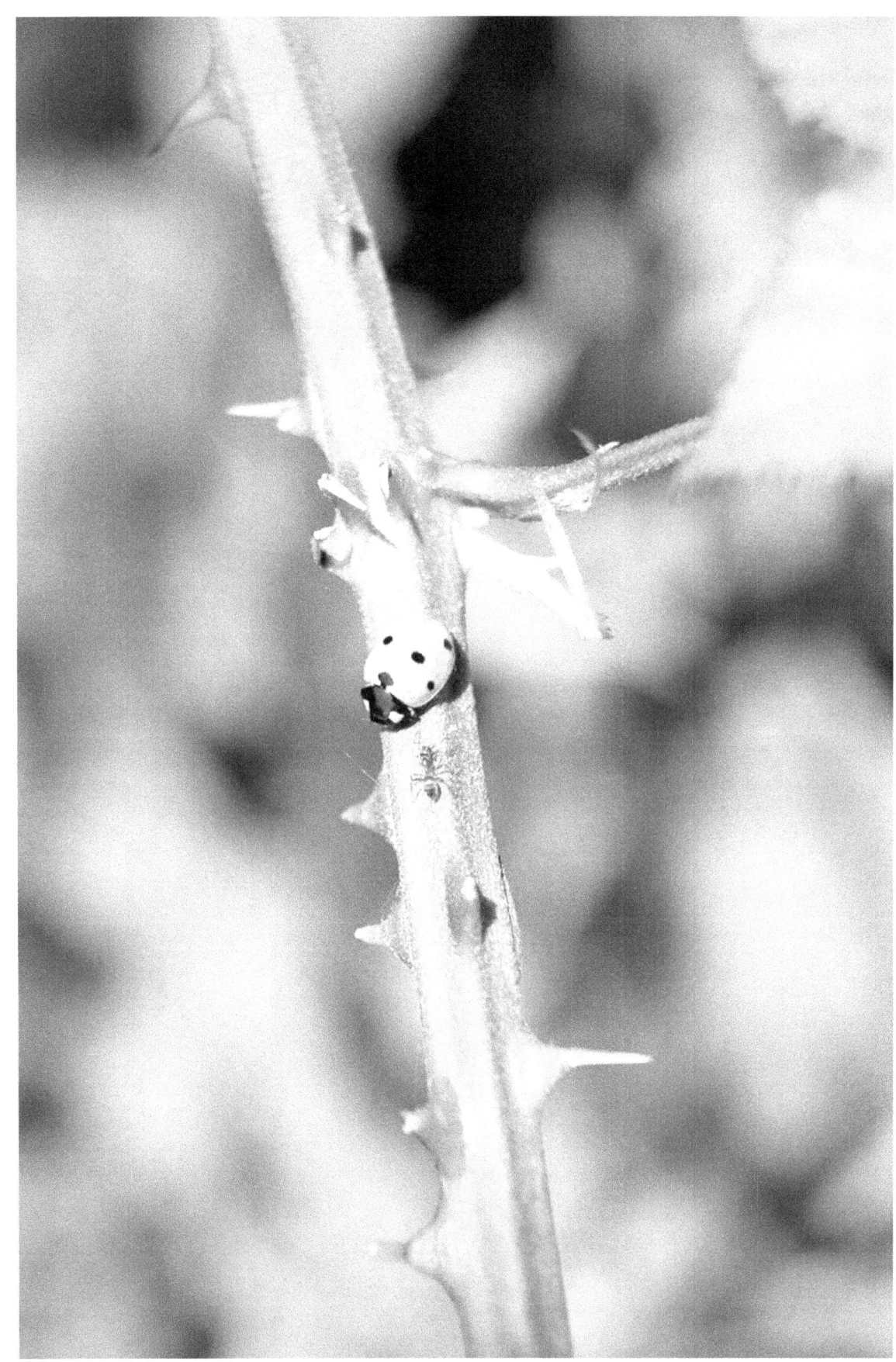

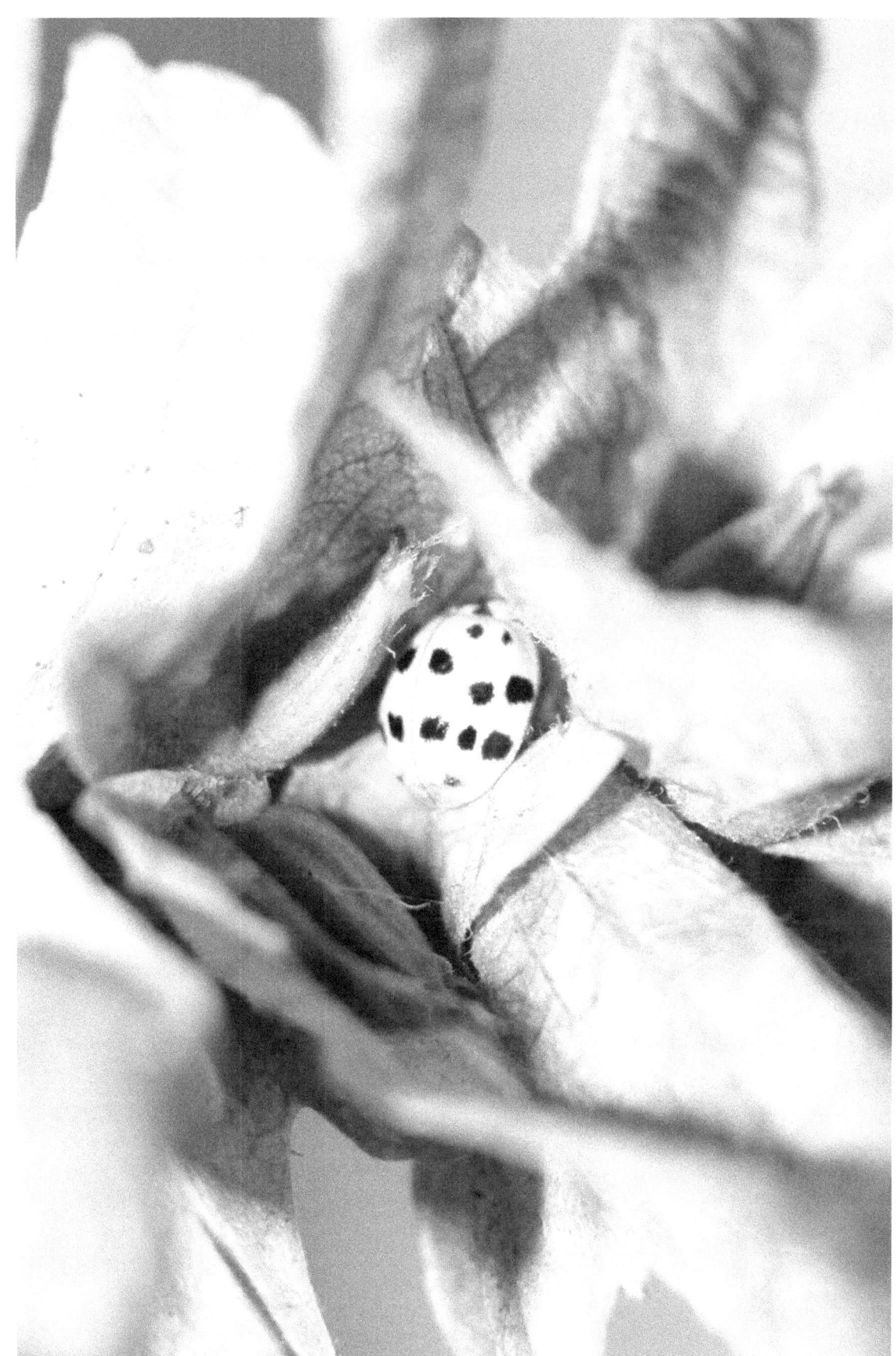

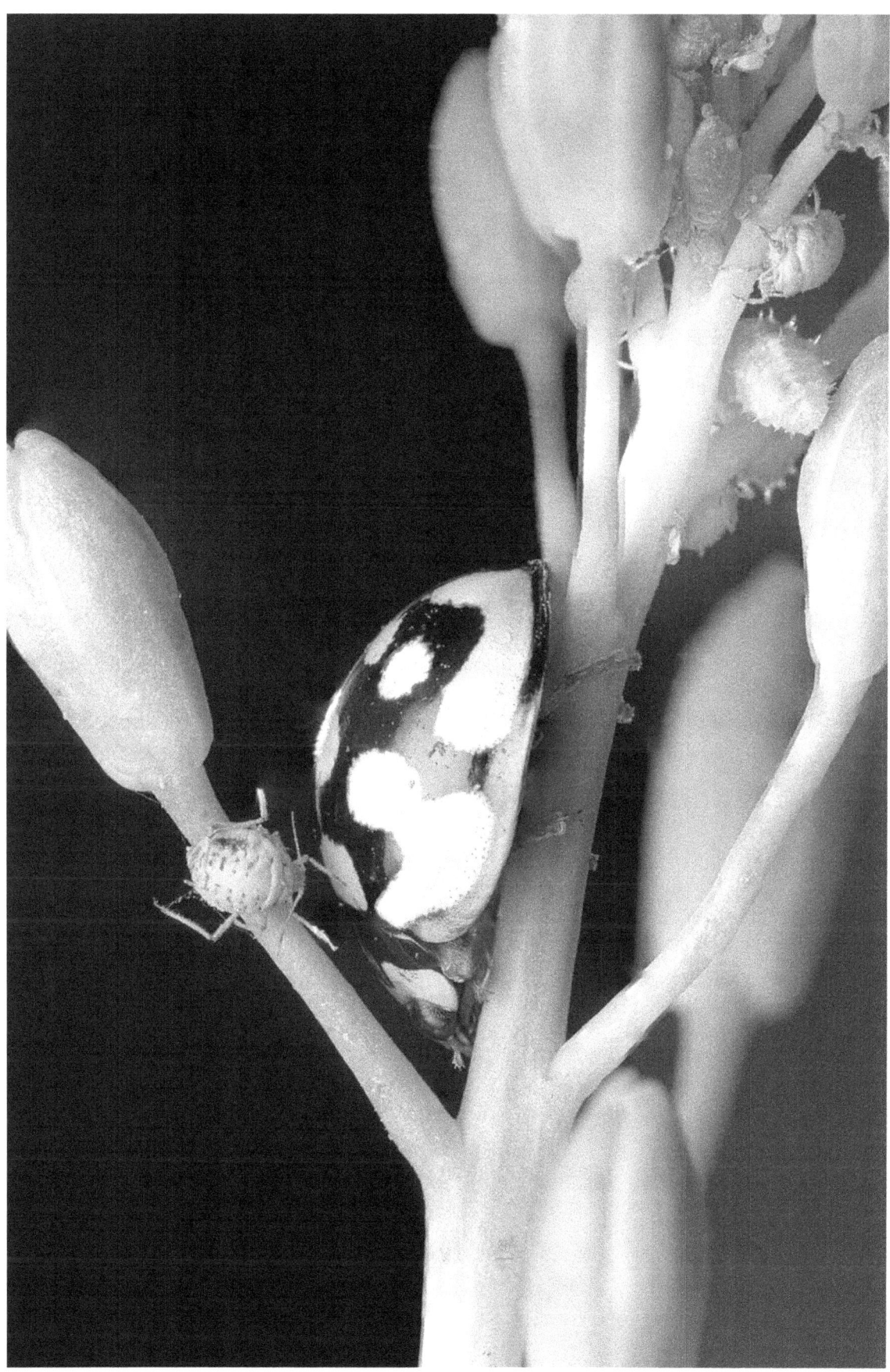

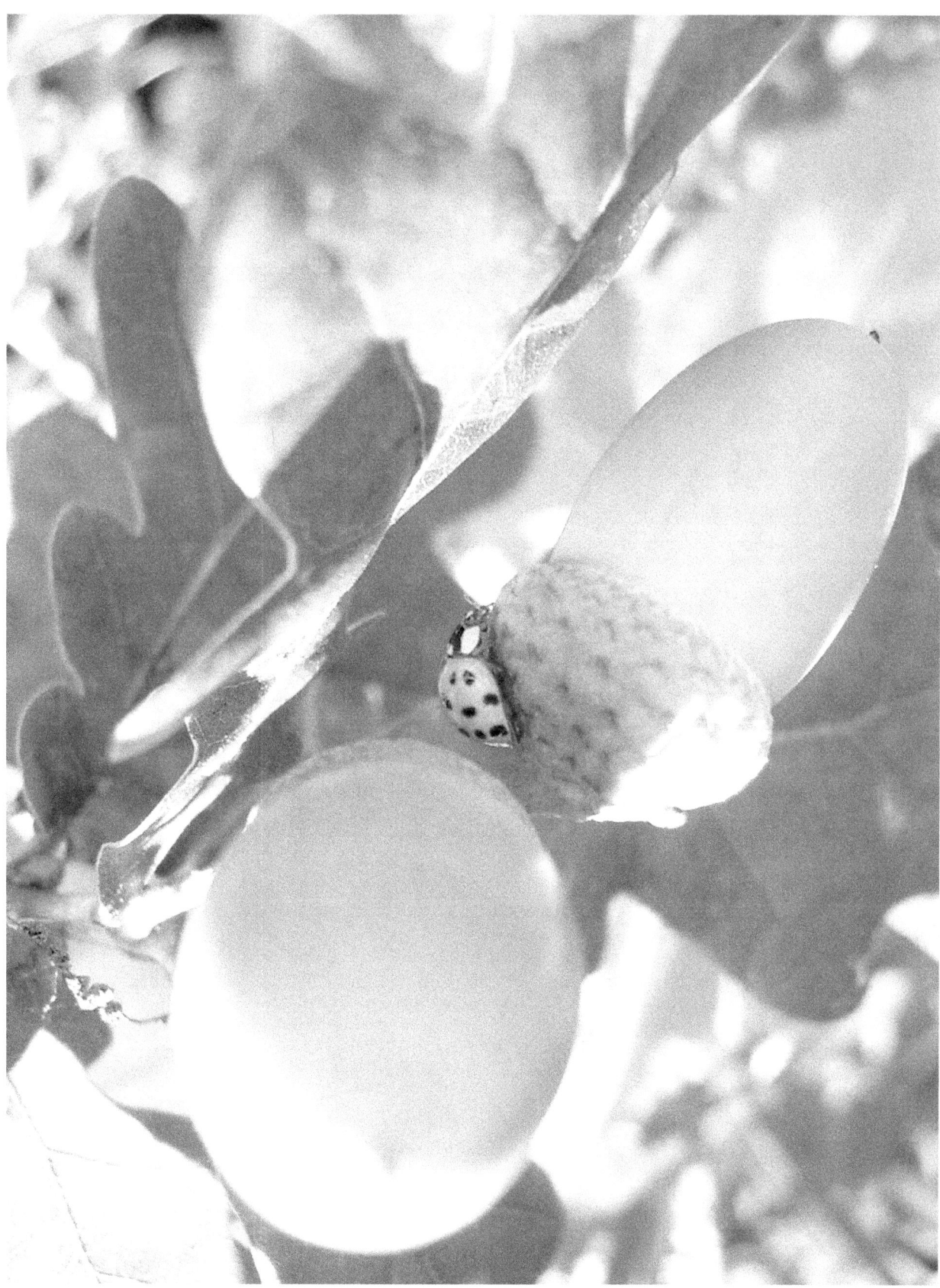

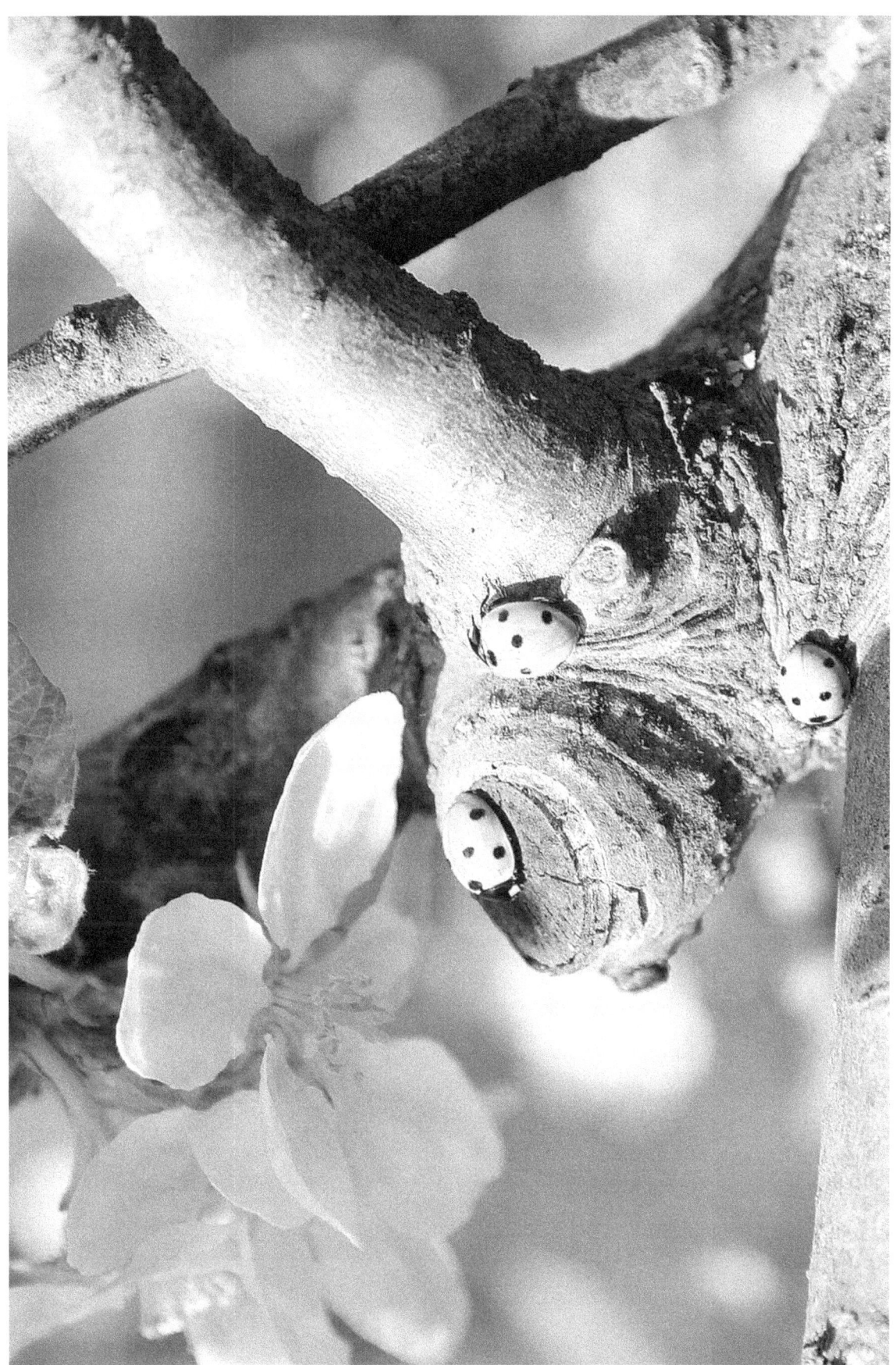

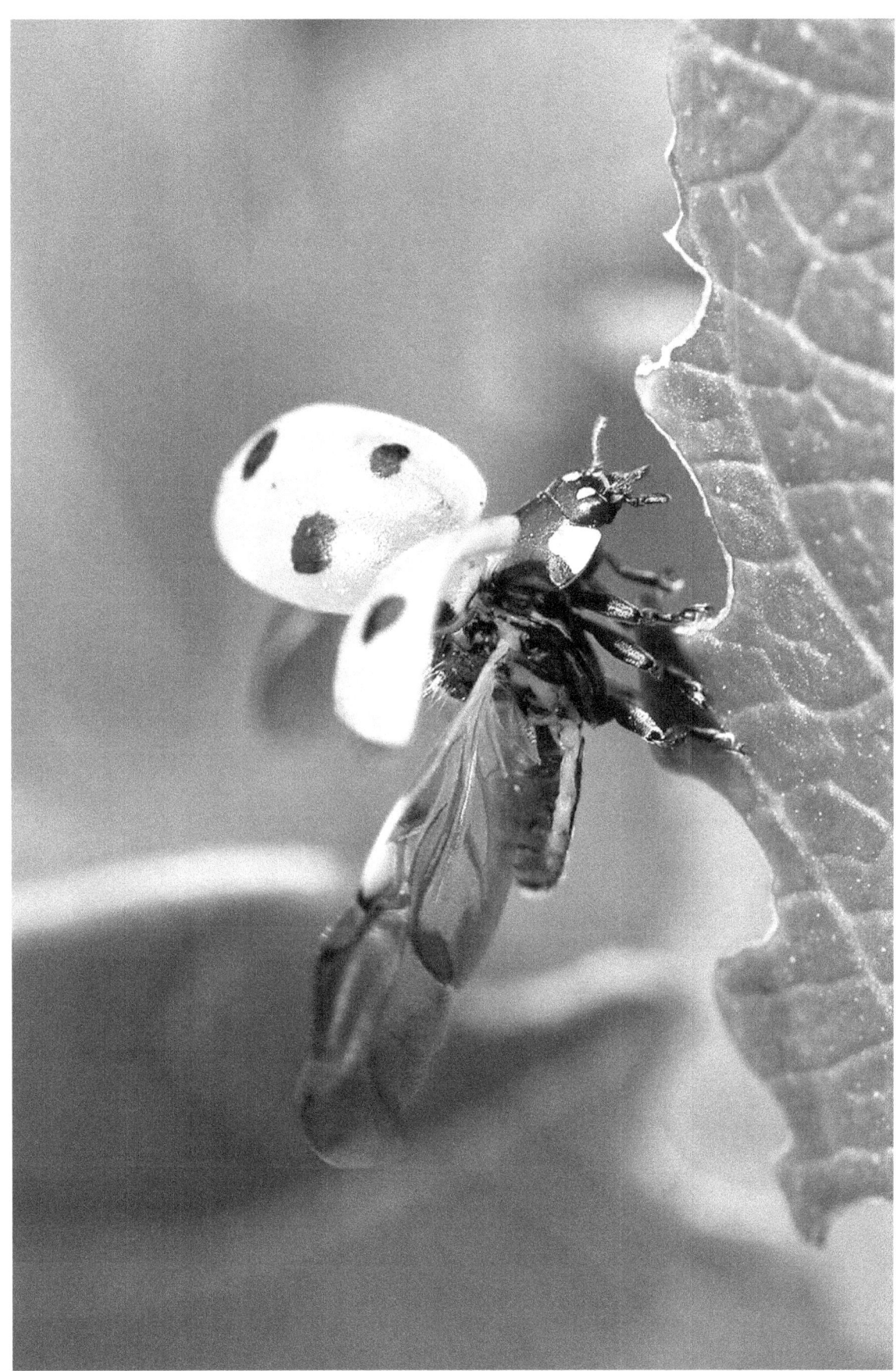

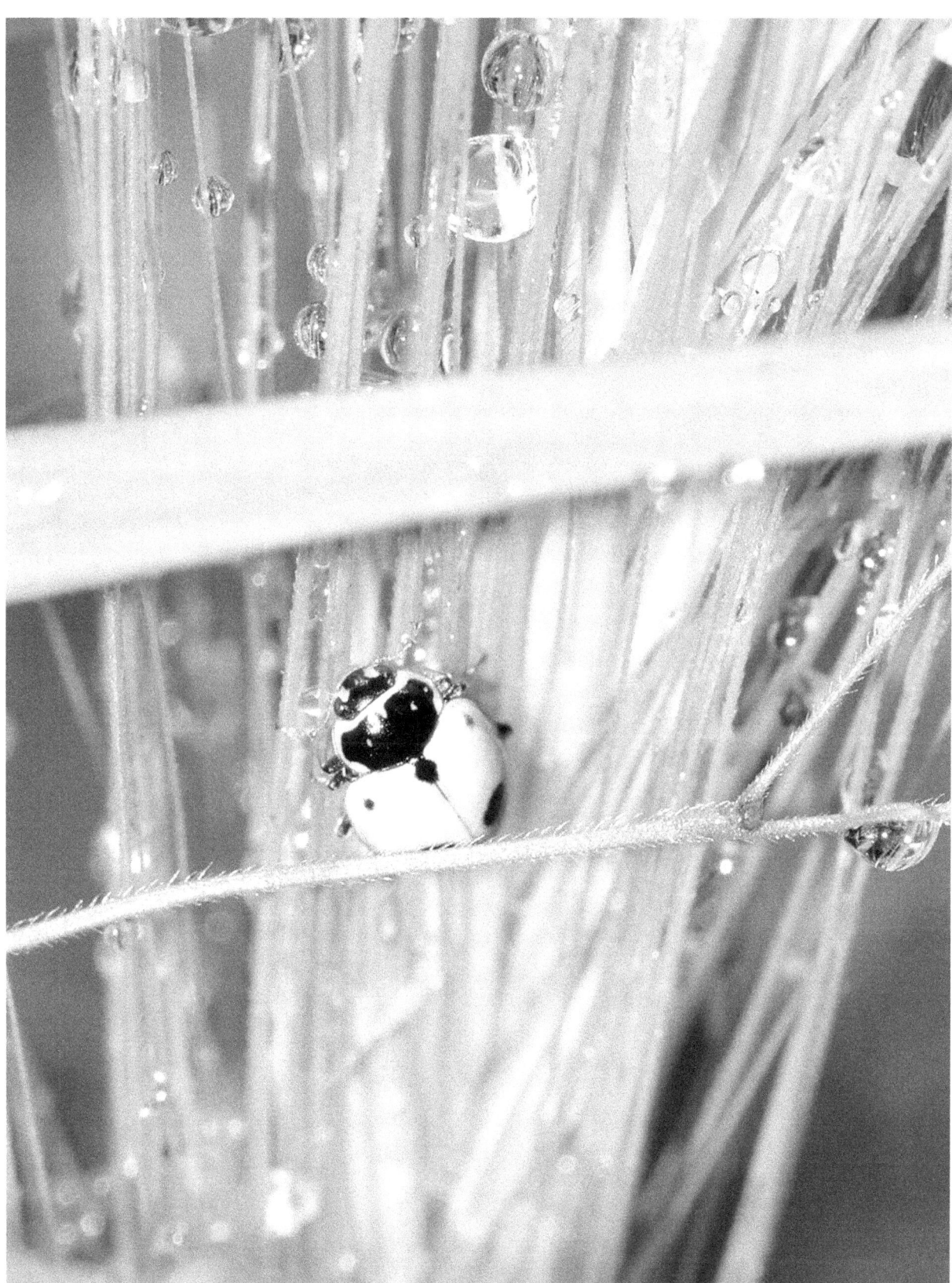

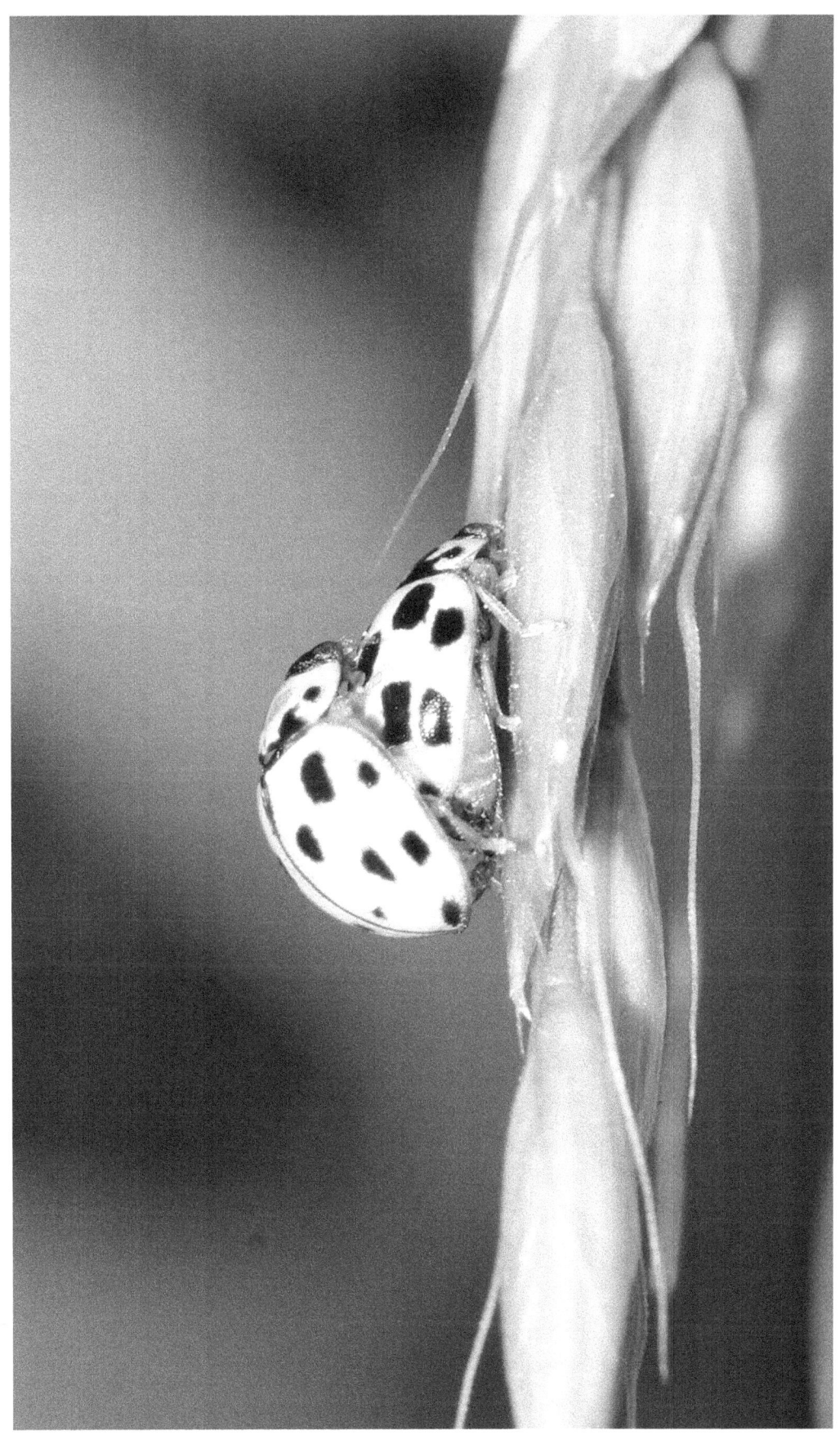

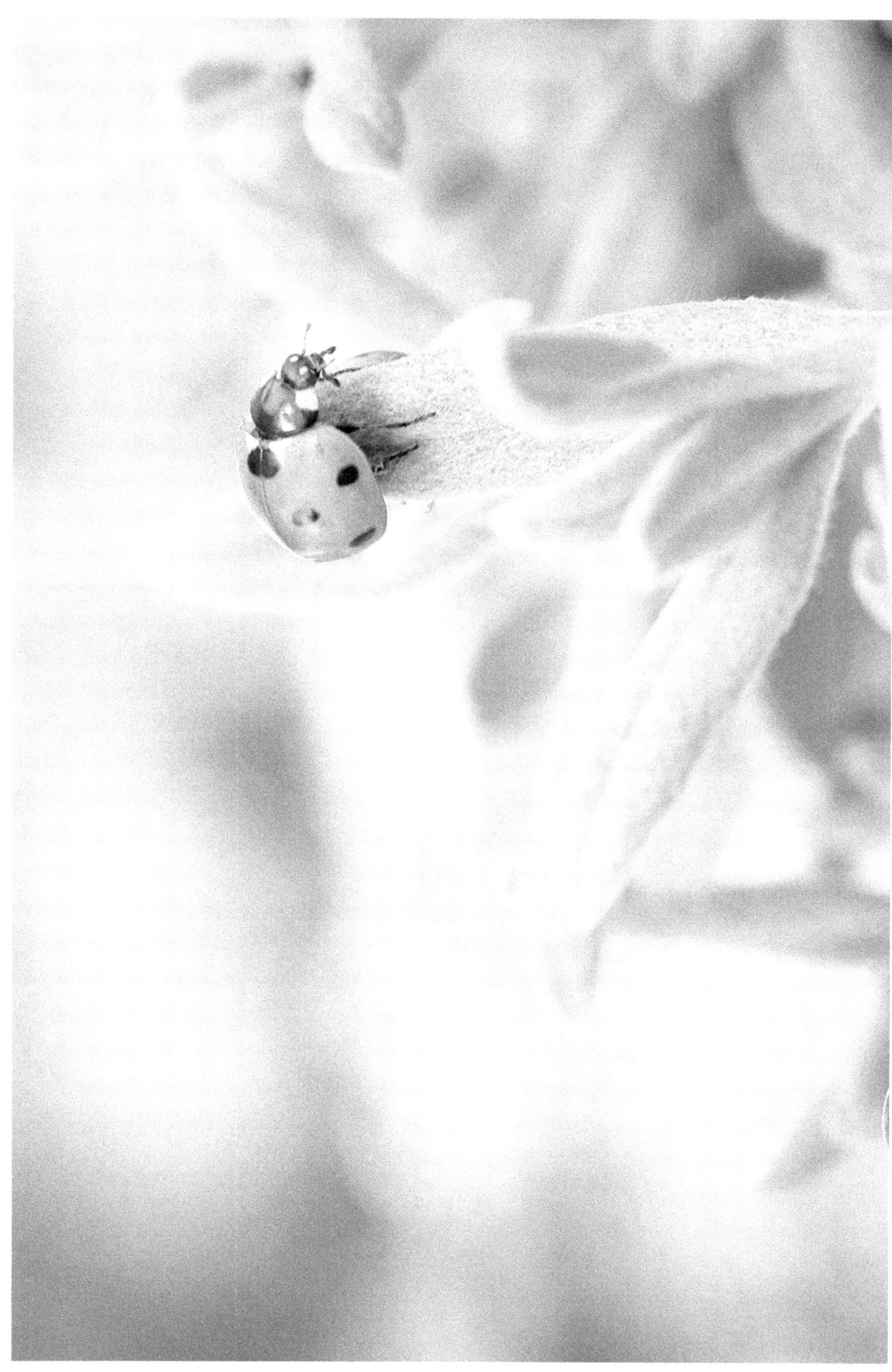

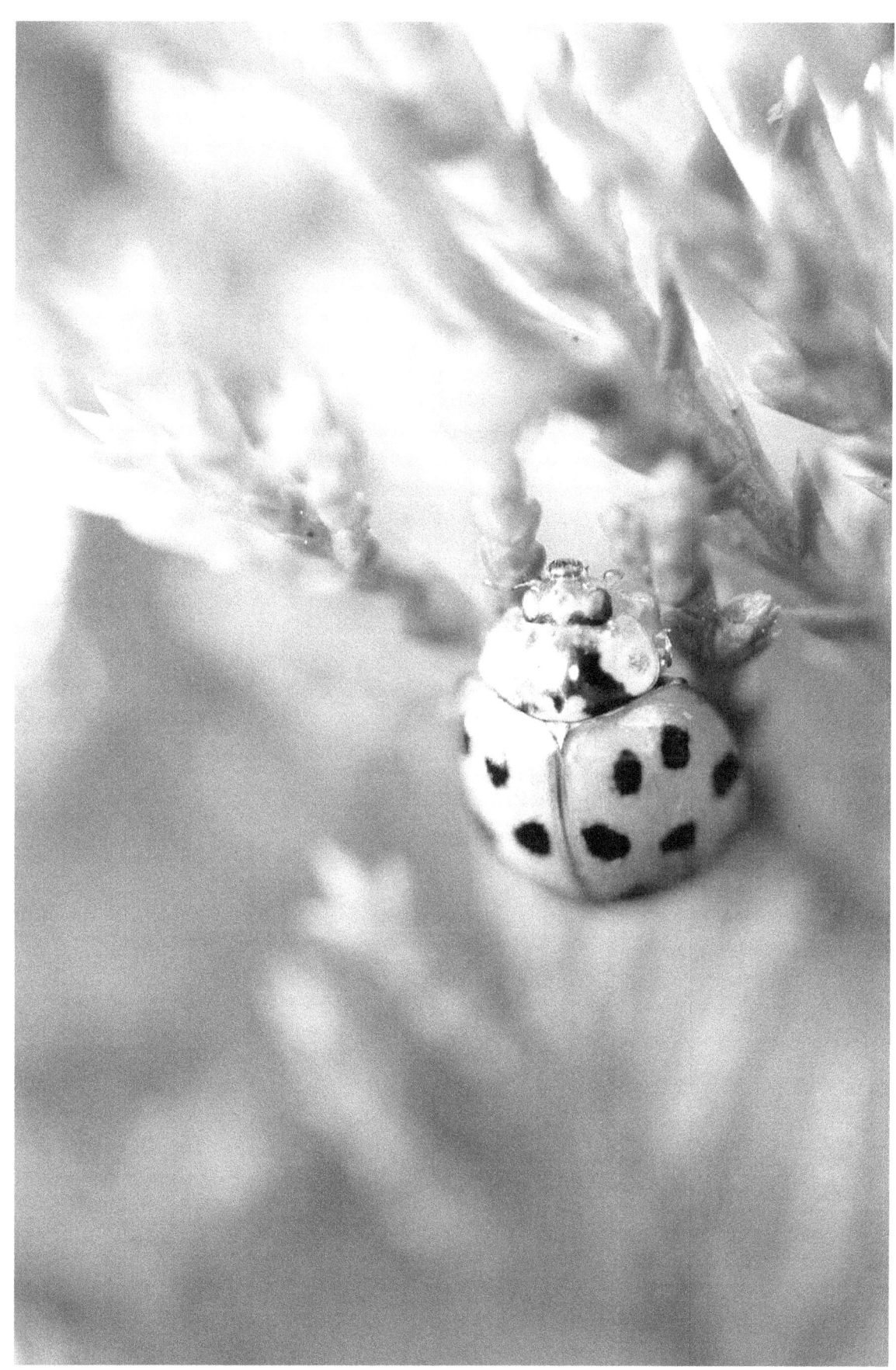

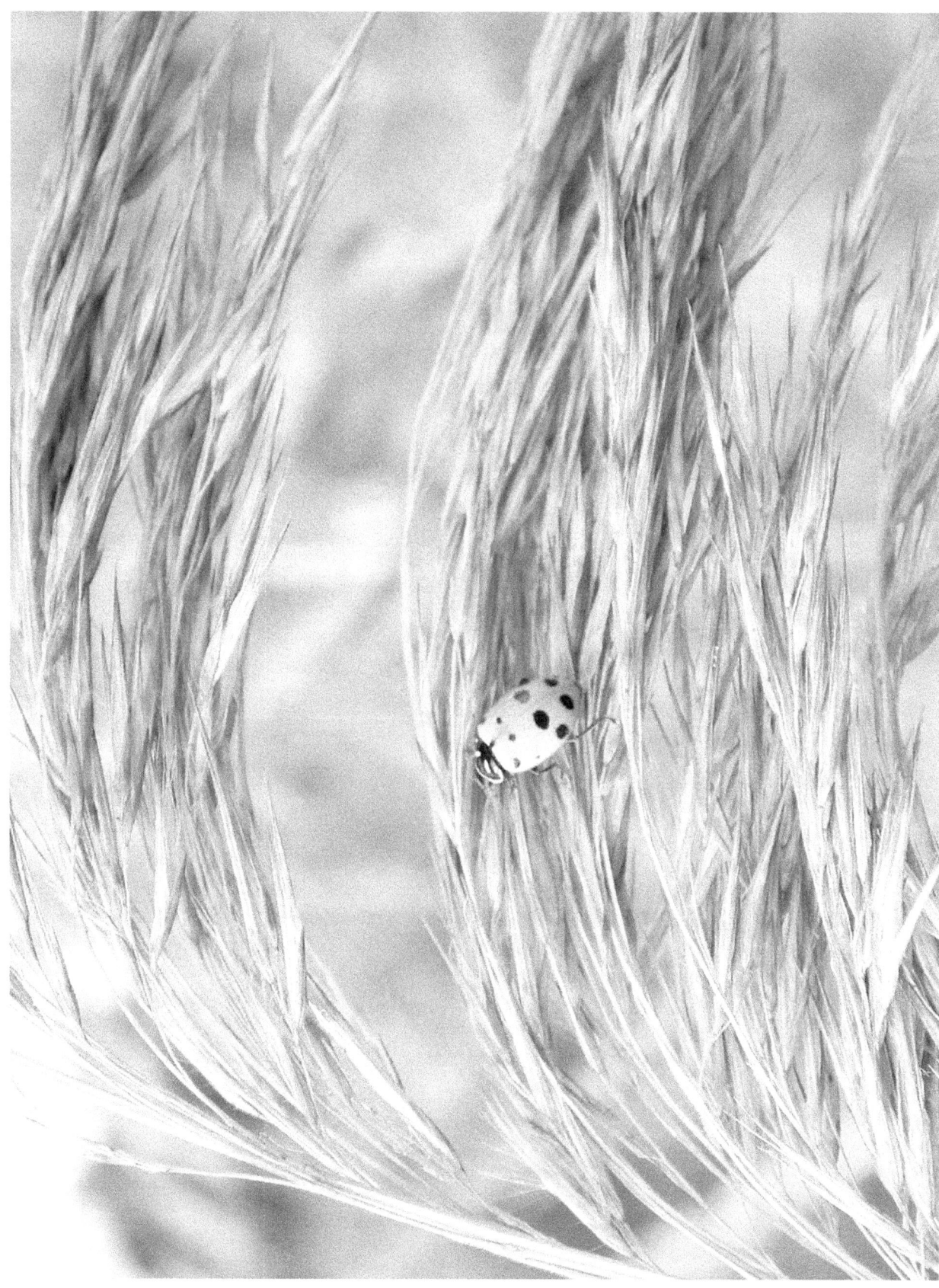

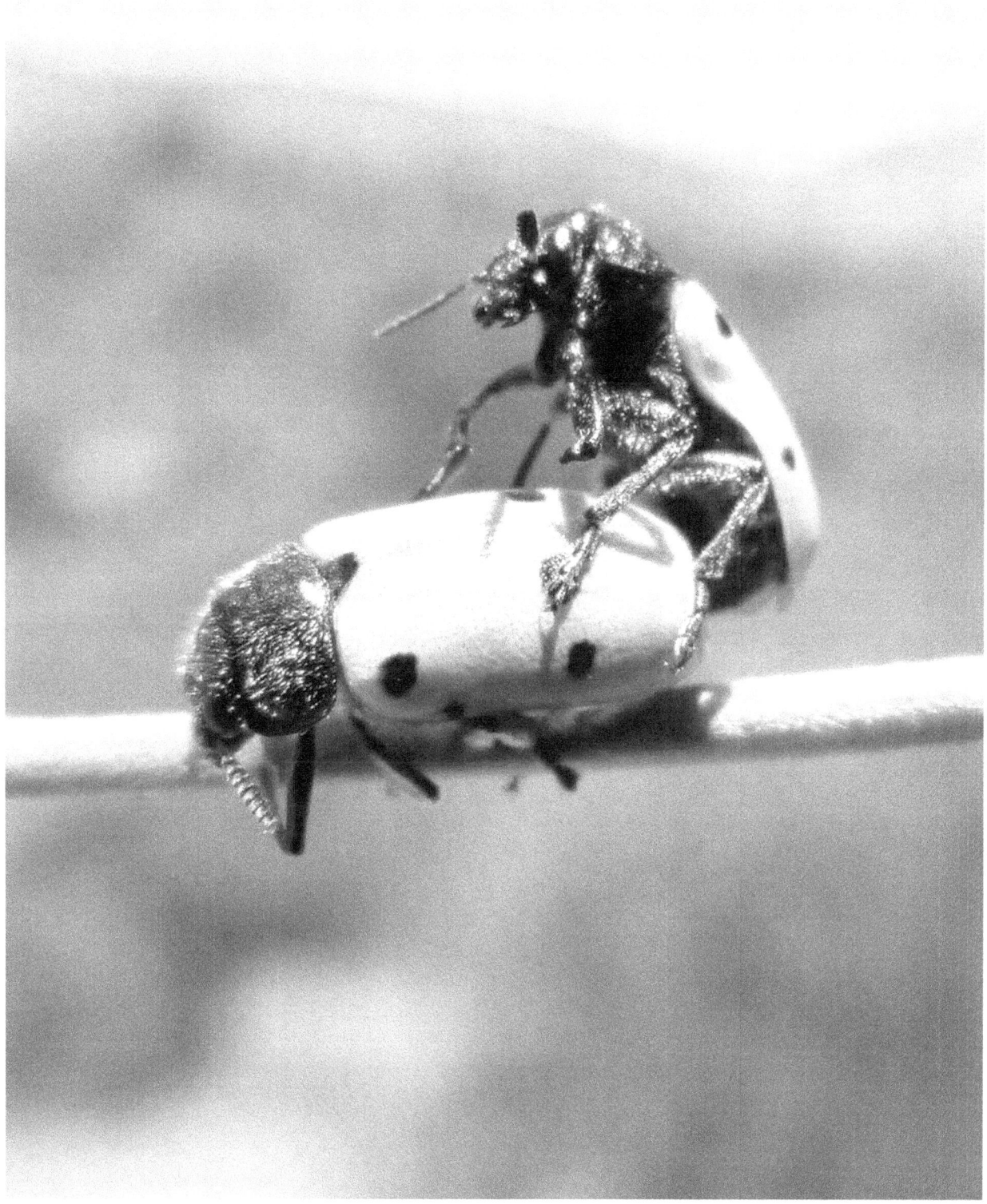

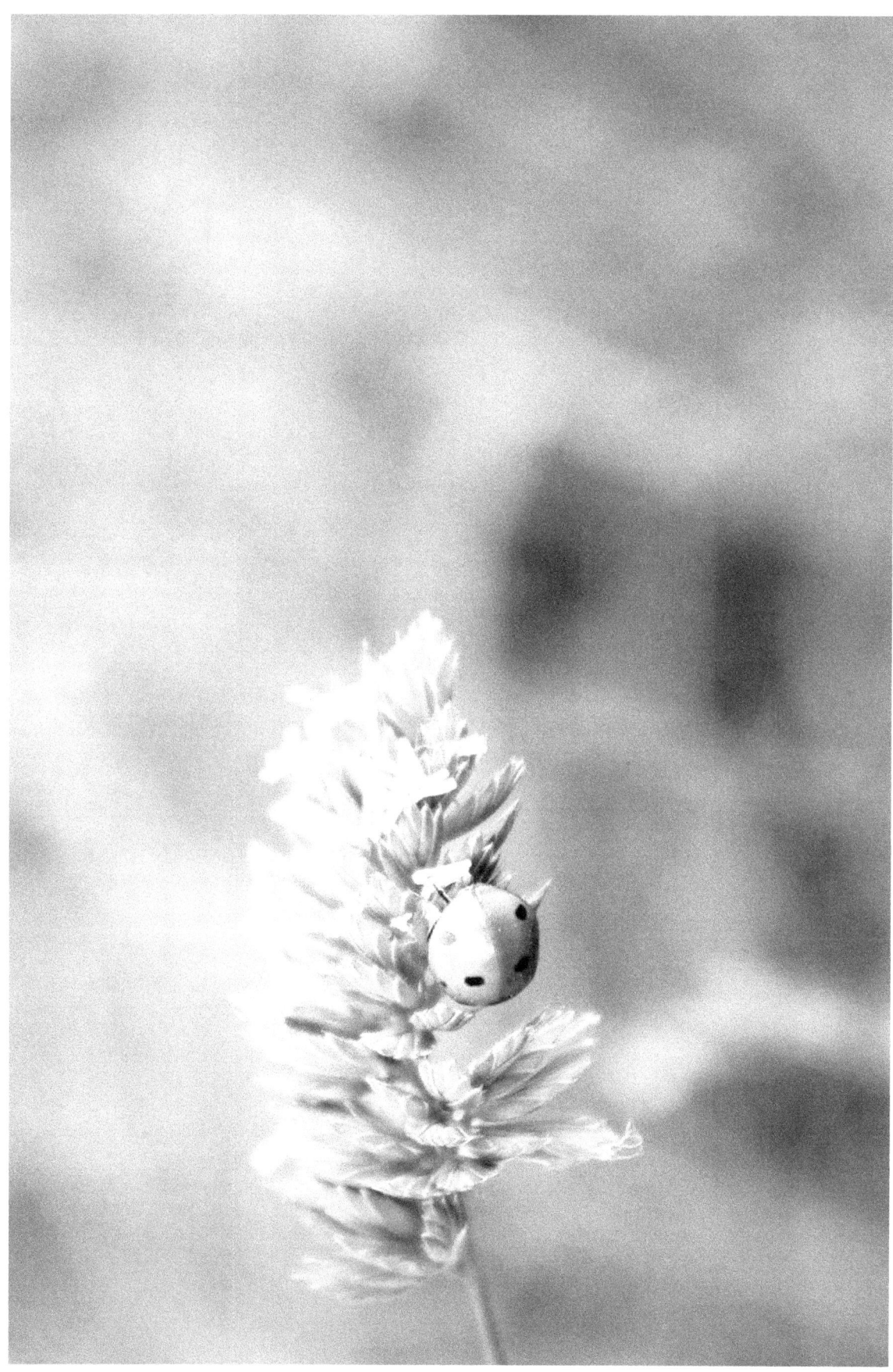

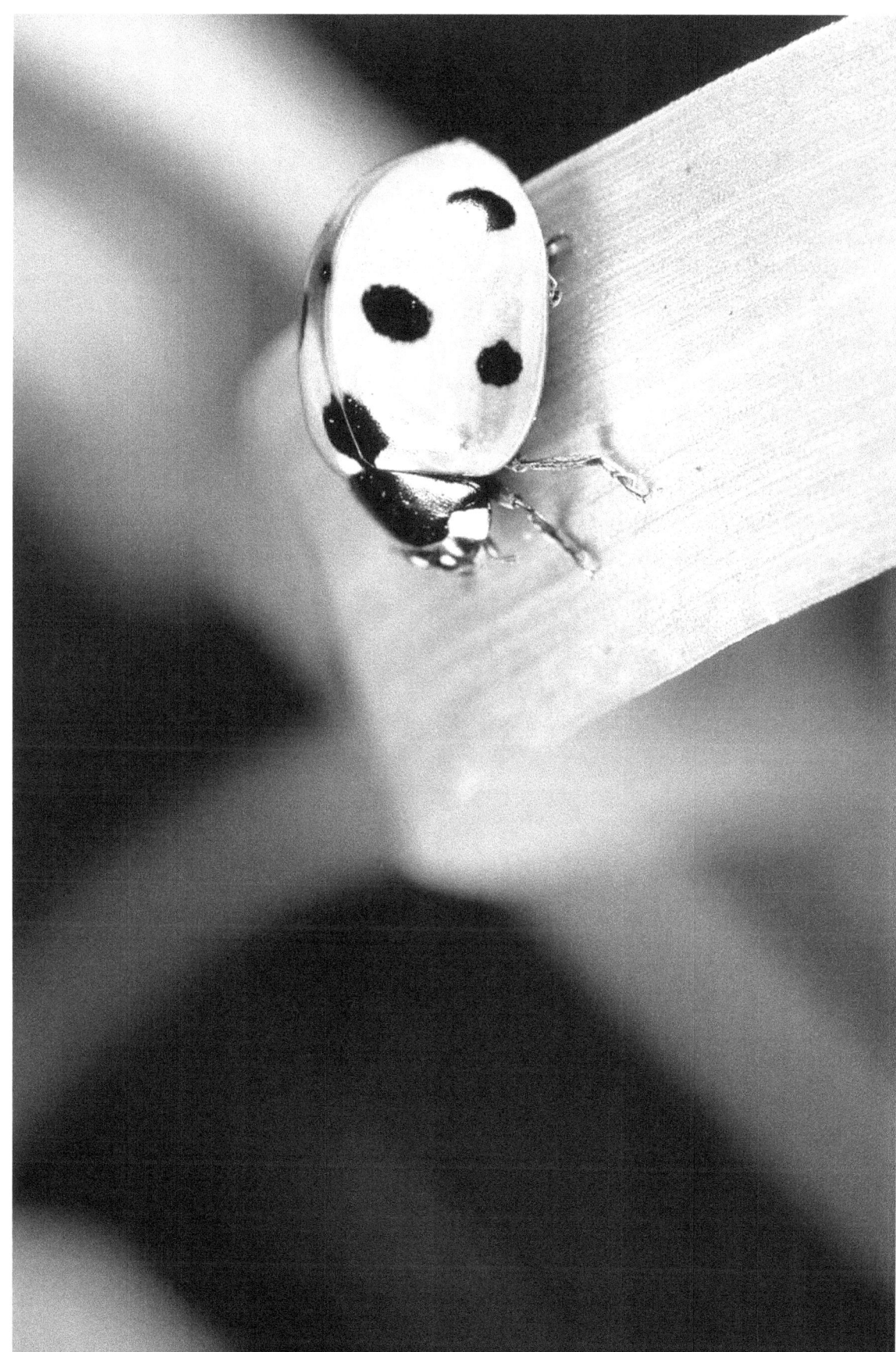

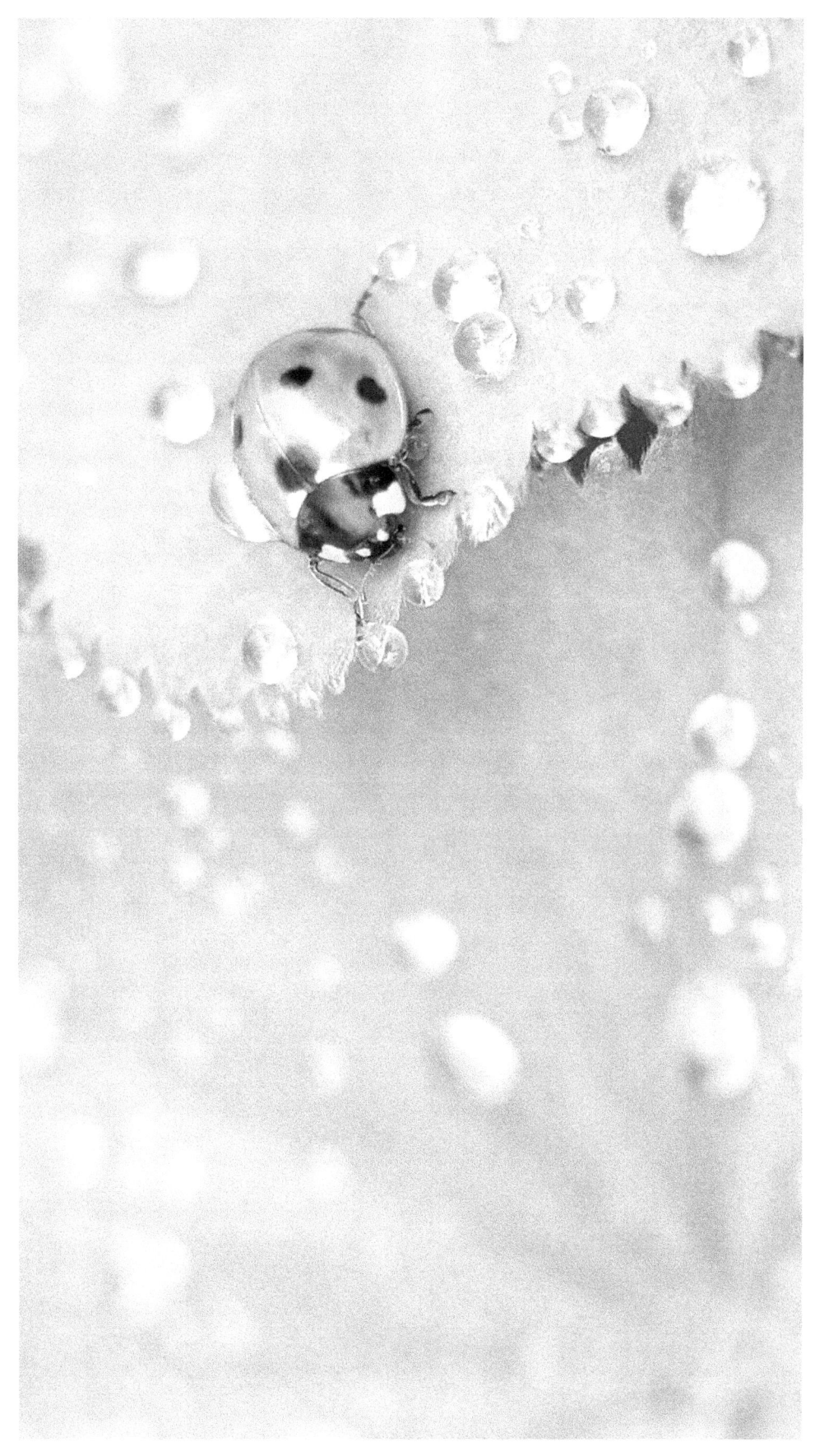

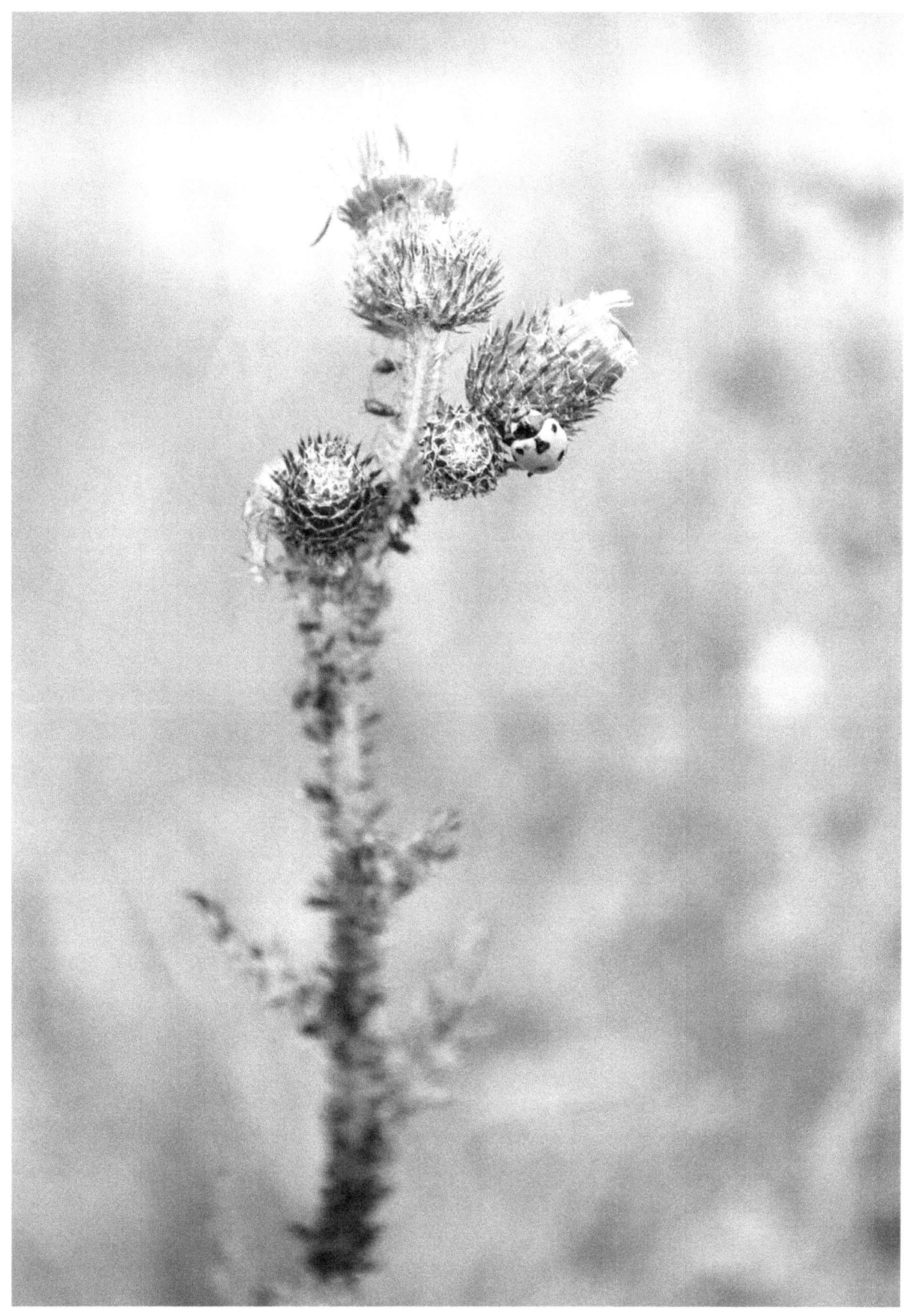

www.ingramcontent.com/pod-product-compliance
Lightning Source LLC
Chambersburg PA
CBHW080554190526
45169CB00007B/2777